The Gatekeepers

To: My Husband with a
great vision & purpose
for our marriage

Date: 1/19/03

From: Your loving wife — I'll
dream with you & work side by
side to see us accomplish this purpose!

The Gatekeepers

*Whatever God Can Get Through You,
He Will Get To You!*

Nate Wolf

insight *i* publishing group
Tulsa, Oklahoma

THE GATEKEEPERS

The Gatekeepers by Nate Wolf
Published by Insight Publishing Group
8801 S. Yale, Suite 410
Tulsa, OK 74137
918-493-1718

Unless otherwise noted, all Scripture quotations are from the New King James version of the Bible. Copyright ©1979, 1980, 1982 by Thomas Nelson, Inc., publishers. Scripture quotations marked Jerusalem Bible are from *The Jerusalem Bible.* Copyright © 1966 by Darton, Longman & Todd, Ltd., and Doubleday & Company, Inc. Used by permission. Scripture quotations marked Amplified are taken from *The Amplified Bible, Old Testament,* Copyright © 1965, 1987 by Zondervan Corporation. *New Testament* copyright © 1958, 1987 by The Lockman Foundation. Used by permission. Scripture quotations marked KJV are from the King James Version of the Bible.

Scripture quotations marked Moffett's, Taylor & Rotherhams, *New American Bible,* Lamsas Translation, were all taken from *26 Translations of the Bible.* Copyright © 1985 Zondervan corporation Grand Rapids, Michigan.

ISBN 1-930027-52-4
Library of Congress catalog card number: 2002101954

Printed in the United States of America

Dedication

This book is dedicated to:

My Lord—For showing me that "can be" comes before "can do."

My Wife & Children—You are my greatest earthly reward.

My Mother—And the many others like her, who dream of giving 90% and living on 10%.

My Staff—For seeing the V.I.S.I.O.N.

Rev. Joe Purcell—For going to Siberia.

Lon—For crying.

John Mason—For believing.

Linda Mason—For "clicking" with Michelle in Florida.

Mike—For saying I could.

Endorsements

"If you're ready to rise up and take your place in the coming Business Age, The Gatekeepers is for you!"

> Carl Sanders,
> Founder/President
> CV Sanders Company

"The Gatekeepers has freed this businesswoman to prosper more than I dare ask or imagine! I will be sharing it with everyone!!"

> Stephanie Richter
> Senior Director
> Mary Kay Cosmetics

"The Gatekeepers has validated the vital contribution of Christian business people to the Body of Christ."

> Todd Aton
> Software Test Leader
> Microsoft Corporation

"The Gatekeepers will ignite the desires God has placed inside of every Christian business leader."

> Ron and Shelley Twiner
> Founders
> Destiny Industrial Consulting

"The Gatekeepers released me in the calling I have known and felt for years."

> Tim Redmond
> Vice President, Intuit Corporation

"I believe that as business leaders grasp the principles in The Gatekeepers it will revolutionize the body of Christ."

> Mark Carpenter
> Real Estate Developer

"As I read The Gatekeepers there was a big "YES!" in my spirit. This book contains fresh and compelling evidence that God is connecting business and church leaders for His purpose."

> Kevin Gerald
> Covenant Celebration Church
> Tacoma, WA

"The Gatekeepers unlocked the secret desires of my heart."

Guy Bennett
Founder
Fine Structures Inc.

"The Gatekeepers will help you dream big, sleep sound, and wake up astonished."

Stephen & Theresa Hurley
Founders
MacTech Inc., Timeline Services Inc., and The Printer Guys

"After reading The Gatekeepers for 45 minutes I received the most creative business idea I've ever had."

Brenda Kay
Design Consultant

Foreword by John Mason

Life is a lot like the game of tennis. Those who don't serve well end up losing. Nate Wolf's book, *The Gatekeepers,* honestly speaks to believers who want God's prosperity to flow through them.

As a Gatekeeper you will soon discover that unless life is lived for others it is not worthwhile. A self-centered life is totally empty. Proverbs says, "Your own soul is nourished when you are kind; it is destroyed when you are cruel." Think about what questions you will be asked at the close of your life on earth. These questions will not be "How much have you got?" but "How much have you given?" Not, "How much have you won?" but "How much have you done?" Not, "How much have you saved?" but "How much have you sacrificed?"

What you give, lives. Richard Browne said, "Whatever God does in your life is not so you can keep it to yourself. He wants you to give it to others." This book will bless you and others as you experience the joy of discovering that whatever God can get through you, He will get to you.

The secret to living is giving.

John Mason

Table of Contents

Introduction

One day not long ago, I sat across the table from a Christian businessman as he openly wept. He was weeping because the insights I'm about to share with you in this book so captured his emotions that he said, "It's like the mysteries of my heart as a Christian businessman have been solved."

Suddenly, I recognized something—the vital necessity for Christian business people to realize their staggering importance in God's plan. As a result, I'm alive to the opportunity of helping Christian business people discover greater meaning for their resources and abilities. Once these unique people begin to recognize their extraordinary abilities and distinct function, they will become Gateways of unimaginable wealth flowing towards the undertaking of world evangelism.

What you currently have in your life has been delivered into your life, in large part, as a result of your expectations. Expectation is a golden key to unlocking God's very best for your life. The Bible uses another word for expectation. It's hope.

Hope is powerful stuff. I have a hope for Christian business people—a confident expectation that God will use them. God is raising these people up to become portals of provision in the most important time of all history. Provision, so that the great commission can be fulfilled and the Lord's return can be hastened. I'm banking on hope. I know the power of faith will take my hope in business people and make it a reality, just as it has to many other hopes during my life.

The Biblical definition for hope is "confident expectation." Hope is not wishful thinking. Hope is not whimsical and fanciful. It's confident. It's expectant. It's being in possession of a clear, confident, internal image of what you will be one day.

Like a skilled navigator, hope literally charts the course for your future destiny. Hope is a guidance system. Without hope, we have no compass to move confidently towards our tomorrows (Rom. 8:23-25). The writer of Hebrews tells us that without hope, faith has no raw material to create better realities in our lives (Heb. 11:1).

I have great hopes for you. When you finish reading this book I want you to be so filled with hope for your future that it will set you in motion. I want you to be so possessed with a sense of opportunity that you'll burn with the desire to act. I want you to so plainly recognize who you are that you'll never doubt it again. You have been give uncommon abilities to gain wealth, to influence commerce in a community, and to mobilize the profits for the Master's purpose (Matt. 25: 15).

You are a Gatekeeper!

Chapter One

Gatekeepers Influence
The Flow of Resources

A few years ago I made my first trip to the nation of Israel. Journeying through the land of the Bible left me with many remarkable impressions. One of the most significant of these insights struck me while I was reflecting on a visit to the old walled city of Jerusalem. In fact, I still have the photo of the image that prompted a major paradigm shift in my thinking.

For hundreds of feet before and after a large stone gateway, there were vendors and businesses of almost every kind possible. You see, Jerusalem's gates are the only major entry points into the old walled city. Hundreds of thousands of people pass through them daily. As a result, they are strategic centers of business activity. At the city gates you can literally purchase everything from olives to insurance policies to cell phones.

Did you know there are over one hundred references to city gates in the Bible? During this moment of reflection, many of them began flooding my memory. However, I was thinking of them all in a new light. I now saw the term "gates" referring to places of business activity. In the land of the Bible, where cities were walled for their defense, the gates were marketplaces. Because so many people had to pass through them they were the most profitable places to conduct business.

That day, at the gates of old Jerusalem, I was impacted with so many powerful images. It was like taking a journey back in time. You could see resources and commodities of every imaginable sort being transported through the city gates. Flour for the bakers and leather for the cobblers were being conveyed on old wooden carts, much as they would have been thousands of years ago.

Even in the modern high tech world we live in, the term gateway still has business ramifications. It often refers to the portal or entry point of a Web site where one can conduct business. Every major Web site has places where you can point and click to do business—they are virtual marketplaces. These days, even people doing business on computers have to enter through gateways.

In the Bible, "city gates" refer to the physical entry points where the resources and supplies flowed into a city. I was seeing everything in a new way. When the book of Proverbs says that, *"by the gateways opening into the city, she (wisdom) wisdom cries out"* (Prov. 8:3, Moffet's Translation) it now meant to me that wisdom could be found in the marketplace—the places where the resources flowed. I realized I could be passing by wisdom every day. Could I previously have been looking for wisdom in the wrong places? After all, wisdom is God's word applied. What better place to apply the word of God than the marketplace?

> *Gatekeepers are the ones who influence the resources and supplies that flow into a business organization.*

When Isaiah gives his last days description of God's people, *"Your gates will stay open around the clock that men may bring to you the riches of the nations"* . . . . (Isa. 60:11, Taylor's and Rotherham's Translation) it now meant to me that God's people could conduct business

19

activities that would gather wealth on a continual basis. All of a sudden, Isaiah's prophecy meant so much more to me. God has an end-time plan for businesses. Do you want to be a part of it? I do.

When you consider the idea of gateways, there is another very powerful idea involved—one that must not be ignored. It is that of a Gatekeeper. Gatekeepers are the ones who determine what comes through the gates. However, in a very real sense, they are the gate itself. Nothing goes through the gate without the participation of a Gatekeeper. Even in modern business and corporate terminology, Gatekeepers are the ones who influence the resources and supplies that flow into a business organization.

For example, on the day of my visit in old Jerusalem there was a group of Israeli soldiers standing on top of the city wall. Although they were protecting the city from attack, they were not the Gatekeepers. The soldiers were not influencing which resources flowed into the city—how much flour and what spices. It was the business people in the city gate who influenced the flow of resources. It was the decision makers in their business organizations that decided what commodities would enter the city. Just as there are Gatekeepers in modern corporations—people who influence the resources and supplies that flow into an organization—in the land of the Bible the business people are the Gatekeepers of the city.

There are Gatekeepers in the land of the Bible. There are Gatekeepers in modern corporations and businesses today. And there are Gatekeepers in God's Kingdom who dramatically influence the flow of resources and supplies into His work.

Even as we've already read in Isaiah's prophecy, there is a shift of wealth taking place today. The people of the earth are bringing wealth to Christian business people who walk in integrity. The Bible prophesies this financial shift and the Gatekeepers, godly business people, have an essential part to play in that exchange of riches. You could dare to be part of the wealth shift. You could dare to be a Gatekeeper.

Now you can understand why the book of Proverbs says that the wise woman's husband, *"is prominent at the city gates as he sits with the Elders of the land"* (Prov. 31:23, New American Bible).

Why did the prominent men, the Elders, these "City Fathers," sit at the city gate? Because they were the influential businesspeople, the Gatekeepers, who influenced the flow of resources that would come into the city. The Gatekeepers are even more important than the gate itself. Gates may do a city little good without godly and competent Gatekeepers. In the same way, business activities may do God's work little good without godly and competent people overseeing those activities.

Decide to be a godly businessperson. Decide to be a competent businessperson. God can't trust us with prominence if we haven't committed ourselves to competence. Decide to be competent in the awesome responsibility God is committing to you.

It is God's plan to empower Gatekeepers because they are a focal point for provision to flow into His work. The book of Proverbs says, *"He who increases his wealth by unjust means amasses it for someone else who will bestow it on the poor"* (Prov. 28:8, Lamsa's Translation and *The Jerusalem Bible*).

Gatekeepers are the point of transfer where improperly gained wealth becomes properly utilized wealth.

There is an old Egyptian proverb that says, "Wealth which comes through the door unjustly will go out the window quickly." Gatekeepers are the windows that unjustly gained wealth will pass through on its way towards higher purposes. Make a decision right now to become a focal point through which resources can flow. Become like the narrow end of a funnel, where resources can be poured out to their greatest usefulness. Dare to become a Gatekeeper.

Chapter Two

Gatekeepers Respond
to God's Ability

*W*hat if I told you there was a special ability from God for Gatekeepers? That God would give certain people the ability to cause wealth to shift hands? Would you want that ability? If you're daring to be a Gatekeeper you would.

Just before George Bernard Shaw died, a reporter asked him this question, "Mr. Shaw, you have visited with some of the world's most famous people. You've known royalty, renowned authors, artists, teachers, and dignitaries from every part of the world. If you could live your life over and be anybody you've ever known, whom would you choose to be?"

Shaw replied, "I would choose to be the man George Bernard Shaw could have been, but never was."

George Bernard Shaw felt he possessed capabilities that he never fully recognized. What if embracing the profound ability of a Gatekeeper begins with simply recognizing it? What you see is what you get? Could it be that simple? Yes, because recognition activates a spiritual law that releases ability.

In His hometown of Nazareth, Jesus had difficulty with people not appropriately recognizing His ability. Did it matter? Let's see. The Gospel of Mark says the people of Nazareth said, *"**He's only** the carpenter."* It then says, *"This proved a hindrance to their believing in Him. **And He was not able** to do any miracle there"* (Mark 6:1-6).

Do you see how powerful recognition can be? Even Jesus was limited by how people viewed Him. To the same degree the people of N a z a r e t h failed to recognize Jesus' ability—they failed to receive it. To the same degree you fail to recognize God's ability for you—you will fail to receive it.

> *If you say, "I'm only a carpenter, I can't be a Gatekeeper," then you will limit God's ability.*

When the people said, "He's only a carpenter, He can't be God's son" it limited Jesus' ability. If you say, "I'm only a carpenter (or whatever your profession may be), I can't be a Gatekeeper," then you will limit God's ability. What you recognize, talk about, and act upon will bring either good or bad results to your life. Refuse to recognize inability—recognize God's ability. Talk about it. Act upon it.

Fred Smith, the founder of Federal Express, put up $4 million of his own money when he started his company in 1971. Fred Smith invested his own money and it persuaded a group of venture capitalists to put over $80 million more dollars into Federal Express. At the time, it was the largest venture capital package ever assembled. Fred Smith recognized his abilities and did something about it. What would happen if you recognized God's abilities and did something about it?

How did Jesus deal with the recognition problem in Nazareth? The gospel of Mark says, *"He traveled about teaching"* (Mark 6:6). Jesus used God's thoughts to educate people about His ability. Begin to use God's thoughts to educate yourself about your Gatekeeper ability. The Bible is a book full of God's thoughts about you.

Paul the Apostle said, *"And God hath set some in the church, first apostles, secondarily prophets,* *thirdly teachers, after that miracles, then gifts of healings, **helps**, governments, diversities of tongues"* (1 Cor. 12:28 KJV).

I had always been taught that "helps" described people who helped anywhere needed in the church. If the floor needed vacuuming, people with the gift of "helps" vacuumed it. That concept always raised these questions in my mind, "Why would the gift of vacuuming be listed with the mighty apostles, those that taught God's word, and the spectacular gifts of miracles and healings? Vacuuming is good, but does it require a supernatural ability to do it?"

Then one day the Holy Spirit quietly whispered in my heart the answer to my questions. The reality He introduced was so stunning, and so new to me, that it took me completely by surprise. To me, it was an absolutely new realization—something I'd never seen before.

This is what He said:

*Helps aren't helpers in the church, **they are Gospel Entrepreneurs that will bring millions of dollars** into the church. You can't do anything significant in the earth without them and* they don't have a purpose for their ability to make money without your role in their life. **You need them and they need you.**

One of the major problems in the church is that **people like them have recognized people like you. However, people like you have not recognized people like them.** Whatever my 'five fold ministers' **will not recognize and equip will lie dormant in the church.** Even though they, for the most part, don't teach and preach the word, **they are just as much ministers as you are, and they are just as called and anointed.**

I am calling you to recognize them and to help them bring meaning to their means.

Finding Confirmation In The Greek

As soon as the realization hit me that the term "helps" was a reference to God's Gatekeepers, I wanted confirmation. After all, the word "helps" did sound like it was referring to what I'd already been told, "helps are just helpers in the church."

So the first place I went for confirmation was the Greek language. Why? The New Testament was originally written in Greek and sometimes there are shades of meaning in the original languages that don't always make it through to the English translations of the Bible. I wondered if there was possibly something about the Greek word translated "helps" that didn't cross over to English very easily.

The Greek word translated "helps" is *antilepsis*. A group of Greek language scholars have compiled a volume of study aides called *The Complete Biblical Library*. According to *The Complete Biblical Library*, *antilepsis* is a Greek compound word that combines two other Greek words. The first of these two Greek words is **anti**, which doesn't mean "opposed or against" as it does in English. In Greek, the word **anti** means "instead of, or in the place of." The other Greek word is the word **lambano**, which means "to take hold of, to support." Therefore *antilepsis* means, **"those who stand in another's place and bring support."**

The Complete Biblical Library also says about the word helps, "Those gifts of helps are not necessarily people in positions of authority. Instead, **they are individuals with resources… which others lack.** Helps therefore, involve the giving and sharing of those resources."

Wow! There it is! "Helps" aren't just helpers, they are people in possession of resources, who share those resources with others. They are God's Gatekeepers. Gatekeepers are God's way of supporting financially all the other operations of the church. Gatekeepers are windows of provision. Gatekeepers influence the resources and supplies that flow into God's kingdom.

> *Gatekeepers are windows of provision.*

Now this was cleaning up some of my, as Zig Ziglar says, "stinking thinking." Gatekeepers were being listed right next to apostles, prophets, and miracles in the Bible. Much of my previous religious background had taught me that business people really weren't "anointed" of God. Couldn't anyone just go out and become a successful businessperson? It doesn't really take a gift from God to do that does it? After all, business people are in the "secular" arena, and preachers are the only ones that are really "anointed" aren't they?

On the contrary, God is asking people to dare to be His Gatekeepers. The word "anointing" is used in the Christian community quite often. Would you like to know what the anointing is? Basically, the word "anoint" means, "to smear with ability."

The anointing is God's ability coming on a person, giving them the ability to do what they couldn't do without it. Just like preachers have God's ability–Gatekeepers have God's ability. It's just a different kind of ability. Have you been smeared with God's ability to be a Gatekeeper?

Here's what Gatekeepers who've been smeared with the ability of God will do: Gatekeepers stand in the Kingdom of God's place in the marketplaces of the world. Gatekeepers take hold of material resources and bring them back to the Kingdom of God. The reason they do is so that there is more than enough to fulfill Jesus' greatest commission, *"Go to all nations"* (Matt. 28:18-20).

If God is asking you to dare to be a Gatekeeper, you can now see why it's so necessary that you recognize who you are. To paraphrase former Boston Celtic Larry Bird, "To me a winner is someone who recognizes his God-given talents and then works his tail off doing something about it." You have the ability to be a key player in God's end game. Do something about it today. Recognize and develop your God-given ability to be a Gatekeeper.

Once again, what is the ability of a Gatekeeper? It is the ability to help all of the other ministries in the Lord's church; to stand in their stead in the market-places of the world and bring back the resources the church needs so that there is more than enough to get the job done. What awesome ability. Start recognizing it today. Say, "it's mine; I have it now." When you look in the mirror each morning say, "There stands a Gatekeeper. I am someone God wants to use to influence the flow of resources into His work."

Now that you're beginning to discover your ability, you're getting on track. But just as Will Rogers said, "Even if you're on the right track, you will get run over if you just sit there." It's time for more action. Let's find out what else Gatekeepers can do . . .

Chapter Three

Characteristics of Gatekeepers

$\mathcal{W}$hat else can Gatekeepers do? How do you know if God is asking you to dare to be a Gatekeeper?

If what you've already read is exciting you, then you may be recognizing the call.

Race cars are built so drivers can "feel" the road. To be successful in the world of automotive racing the drivers say, "you must listen to what the road is saying." The drivers must be sensitive to the signals that are picked up by the tires and transmitted to the controls. God has built you to "feel" your assignment. What are you sensing right now?

In the music world there is a principle called "harmonic resonance." If you were to put two perfectly tuned pianos on opposite ends of a concert hall, and then play the E note on one of them, can you guess what might happen? The corresponding E note on the other piano, all the way across the hall, would begin to resonate the same note without anyone playing it. That could be what's happening to you right now. As you're reading about the Gatekeeper, something's resonating on the inside of you—just like the piano in the concert hall.

Certain challenges attract certain people. What kind of astronauts would NASA have attracted for the moon shot if they would have asked, "Who wants to be the second man to go half way to the moon?" Instead they asked, "Who wants to be the first man to walk on the moon?" Neil Armstrong was attracted to the challenge.

When Mary Kay Ash, founder of Mary Kay Cosmetics, wanted to borrow $12 from a friend to attend a sales convention, the friend told her she'd be better off spending the money to buy shoes for her children, instead of wasting it on some dream. Regardless of the opposition, the challenge of sales continued to attract Mary Kay. She since has awarded many pink Cadillacs to those who are attracted by the same challenge.

When NFL running back Herschel Walker was in junior high school, he wanted to play football but his coach told him he was too small. The coach instead advised Herschel to go out for track. Instead of taking the advice of the coach, Herschel undertook a training regimen to build muscle size and strength. A few years later, he won the Heisman Trophy. Herschel Walker was attracted by the challenge football represented.

Are you attracted by the challenge of becoming a Gatekeeper? There are several other distinctions that can help identify those God is asking to rise to the Gatekeeper challenge. Let's discover some more of these distinguishing characteristics. If you have some or all of them—pay close attention—you may be reading about yourself.

First of all, Gatekeepers have recognized their God-given ability as Gatekeepers and consistently reaffirm their calling with their own words.

I covered the importance of recognition earlier; however, never underestimate the power of recognition to produce great results in your life. Mike Murdock says, "What you fail to recognize you will fail to celebrate. What you fail to celebrate you will fail to enjoy." Everyone who has been successful at what God has asked them to do in life, has recognized their assignment, and has constantly reaffirmed it with the words of their mouth.

Jesus used the phrase "I am" over forty times in the Gospel of John. Jesus knew who He was and He constantly reaffirmed it with the words of His mouth. What if Jesus hadn't known who He was? What affect would that have had on the world?

It is not arrogant to verbally reaffirm you are a Gatekeeper. True humility won't deny a reality. True humility is acknowledging who you really are. Humility is a pathway to grace. *"God gives grace to the humble"* (1 Pet. 5:5). If you want grace for your assignment you must recognize your assignment and talk about it. Doing so could have an affect on your world.

Secondly, Gatekeepers have special abilities that serve them both in the kingdom of God's organizations and in the world's business organizations. Although they may seemingly experience more success in one realm, Gatekeepers are gifted in both realms.

Gatekeepers are called by God to operate in both the church and the marketplace.

Gatekeepers are called by God to operate in both the church and the marketplace. God never asks somebody to do something without giving them ability to do it; therefore, they have the ability to function in these two arenas. They bring the resources of one arena into the other. Therefore, they must possess uncommon ability to operate appropriately in both places.

As a pastor, I am often amazed at how seemingly easily some of the Gatekeepers I know operate in the business arena. It's like they were engineered for it. I often ask them, "How did you know to do that?" They frequently respond, "I don't know—I just knew." Where I am awkward, they are fluid and operate with ease. Gatekeepers are gifted in business.

In addition, God's Gatekeepers are also gifted in the church. It's as though they can readily flow from one arena to the other whenever necessary. In order to shift wealth from one realm to the other, they must be competent in both realms.

Gatekeepers cannot fully enjoy fruitfulness in one place without fruitfulness in the other. The primary purpose for their success in the marketplace is so that they can benefit the church. So they must be readily able to function in both the marketplace and the church. To the Gatekeeper it is all really only one realm—they are a bridge between two worlds.

Next, Gatekeepers have a special ability to be "wealth creators." They know and are learning even more ways to produce large amounts of assets. Because of God's pronounced ability in their lives, they can do so without being limited by the world's systems of wealth acquisition.

Seemingly, Gatekeepers have a special ability to create wealth. They're fascinated with means of producing income. When most people are thinking about having one source of income you will often hear Gatekeepers referring to "income streams."

Because Gatekeepers are called by God to give resources, they're going to have to get them somewhere. As Dr. E.V. Hill said, "Whatever God can get through you, he will get to you." Nowhere does this truth apply more readily than to the Gatekeeper. Because God can get resources through His Gatekeeper, He will get resources to His Gatekeeper. God leads Gatekeepers to resources so they can fulfill their destiny.

Gatekeepers have an ability to tap resources so they can give beyond the norm. They don't just have good intentions to give, they are continually searching for more ways to give even more. Gatekeepers live to give.

Gatekeepers must possess resources in order to give them. As Margaret Thatcher said, "No one would remember the Good Samaritan if he'd only had good intentions. He had money as well."

Multi-millionaire and steel baron Andrew Carnegie said, "The sole purpose of being rich is to give away money."

Some people dream of giving 10% of their income away. Gatekeepers dream of living on 10% and giving 90% away. Gatekeepers aren't just dreaming about it either, they're waking up everyday and doing something about it.

Finally, Gatekeepers are also very capable of working with ministries and churches, which produce transformed lives through God's word and Spirit, just as they are capable of working with businesses, which produce improved lives through various products and services.

Just dropping a check into the offering plate isn't the end-all with Gatekeepers. They usually have other spiritual gifts they long to exercise. They want to grow and be used by God in other areas—although not at the expense of their ability to give. Gatekeepers want to roll their sleeves up and get involved in the work of the church.

Remember, everyone in the marketplace isn't always nice, truthful, and operating in integrity. Gatekeepers must confront that not so glamorous marketplace everyday. They're trying to buy, sell, manage, and motivate all day long.

As a result, being involved in churches and ministries is very therapeutic for Gatekeepers. When they're not out there in the trenches of the business world, their involvement in the church brings an element of wholeness to their lives. When Gatekeepers are involved in the church, they're getting their spiritual batteries charged for their next big business deal.

> *When Gatekeepers are involved in the church, they're getting their spiritual batteries charged for their next big business deal.*

Does this sound like a little bit of a balancing act? Like there might be a little stretching and tension involved? Sometimes there is, but Gatekeepers are well suited for the two worlds they live in. Often, one of the greatest feelings of encouragement they find, is just to know the stretching they feel, the tension from being pulled between two worlds, is normal.

Do some of these things resonate in your heart? Can you see yourself in any of these distinguishing characteristics? If you aren't sure yet, don't give up. You're about to learn even more of the extraordinary abilities of Gatekeepers.

Chapter Four

Distinguishing Characteristics of Gatekeepers

*W*ill you allow me to stretch your imagination for a moment? I want to help you start thinking bigger. Paul the apostle said, *"God is able to do superabundantly above all you could dare think"* (Eph. 3:20, Amplified Translation). The bigger we think, the bigger God must act to surpass our thinking.

The richest man in the world reportedly has assets totaling more than $90 billion dollars. Can you imagine having that much money? Let me help you. If you made $100,000 every year, and never spent any of your money, it would take you 900,000 years to save $90 billion.

One of the most well paid athletes in the U.S. reportedly made $40 million during the year preceding his retirement. If he never spent any of his money, it would take him 2,250 years to save $90 billion dollars.

A man who had $90 billion, spending $250,000 on an automobile, would equal a man who had $100,000 spending .27 cents on an automobile. To a billionaire a quarter of a million dollars is like change lying in an ashtray.

The richest man in the world spent $35 million to build his home. Before you say "wow", listen to this. A man who had $90 billion, spending $35 million on a home, would equal a man who had $100,000 spending $38.80 on a home. To a billionaire $35 million is like ordering pizza and renting a couple of DVDs for the evening.

If you think billionaires are the only ones who deal in big amounts, let's look at God. Solomon's temple would have been worth more than $500 billion dollars in modern currency. If you made $100,000 per year, and didn't spend any of it, it would take you five million years to save $500 billion. God deals in bigger amounts than anybody!

To my knowledge, the richest man in the world doesn't serve Christ. He isn't a Gatekeeper—someone who influences the flow of resources and supplies into God's work. What would happen if someone who was a Gatekeeper started to tap into God's ability? What if God, who's the biggest of the big—the Most High—the King of Kings, gave them special ability to get and give money? The potential outcome stretches my imagination. How about you?

Gatekeepers have that ability—the ability to get and give money. Paul the apostle says, *"we have gifts differing… he that exhorteth, on exhortation:* **he that giveth, let him do it with simplicity;** *he that ruleth, with diligence"* (Rom. 12:6-8).

The book of Romans contains a list of seven different spiritual gifts. Some of them, such as prophecy or teaching, are more familiar to those in the Christian community. But did you know that giving is a spiritual gift?

Every Christian should be a giver. Jesus said, *"It's more blessed to give than to receive"* (Acts 10:35). Every Christian should tithe and give offerings (Malachi 3:8-10). However, the book of Romans clearly states there is definitely a special gift of giving.

In Romans Paul says, *"Having then gifts differing"* and then goes on to list seven gifts. That means not everyone has the gift of giving. Every Christian should be a giving person. Every Christian should tithe and give offerings. However, not every Christian has the gift of giving.

The spiritual gift of giving is a unique ability, given only to some Christians, granting them a special expertise in giving. This aptitude empowers them to give above and beyond what is expected of other Christians. The book of Romans says this spiritual gift is given, "according to the grace of God." So one cannot earn this gift—it comes as a result of God's grace. However, one can receive this gift.

The Greek word translated as gift in Romans twelve is *charisma*. Kenneth Wuest, in

> *Gatekeepers impart, and are in a state of readiness to impart, their earthly possessions in an uncommon, special way that exceeds the common amounts, measure, or method of other forms of giving.*

his *"Word Studies in the Greek New Testament,"* says this word means, "extraordinary powers distinguishing certain Christians and enabling them to serve the church of Christ." He goes on to say, "the reception of these gifts is due to the power of divine grace operating in their souls by the Holy Spirit."

Gatekeepers are extraordinary givers. It is what distinguishes them more than anything else. They are people who serve the church by giving in an extraordinary fashion.

According to Noah Webster's 1828 edition of the *Dictionary of the English Language*, the word "extraordinary" means "uncommon, special, beyond or out of the common order or method, and exceeding the common degree or measure."

The word "giveth" used in Romans twelve means "to impart of one's earthly possessions." The concept of being "ready to impart" can also be derived from the word "giveth."

Gatekeepers impart, and are in a state of readiness to impart, their earthly possessions in an uncommon, special way that exceeds the common amounts, measure, or method of other forms of giving.

Paul goes on and says that Gatekeepers should give *"with simplicity."* That means they give with sincere and pure motives. It means their extraordinary gifts should have no strings attached—that they should be free from pretense, full of honesty, and in possession of an open heart. It means that they will desire no disproportionate attention, incentive, or bestowing of privilege for their liberal giving. Gatekeepers' hearts simply burn with fervency for churches, ministries, and the preaching of the gospel to be strengthened through their willing acts of obedience and gifts that exceed the norm.

In order to give in a way that exceeds the norm, one must have resources that exceed the norm. Gatekeepers have an uncommon ability to gather and create wealth for the purpose of giving. These are not natural abilities—they are supernatural abilities. Remember Kenneth Wuest states this gift is "due to the operation of the Holy Spirit in a person's soul."

Gatekeepers are benefited greatly when they cultivate a relationship with the Holy Spirit. A relationship with the Holy Spirit is a golden key in the hand of a Gatekeeper that can open new realms of wealth. The Holy Spirit will give the Gatekeeper an edge in the marketplace. The Holy Spirit could give a Gatekeeper one idea that would be worth millions, even billions, of dollars.

The man who created the design for the "earth mover," a large piece of heavy construction equipment, says that the Holy Spirit gave him the idea for the equipment's design one morning after rising early. He sketched the idea on a memo pad lying on his night-stand and later developed it into a series of multi-million dollar designs.

Every Gatekeeper is equipped with the gift of giving. It is the most distinguishing characteristic they possess. It gives them the ability to influence the resources and supplies that flow into God's work.

According to Paul, all of the gifts listed in Romans twelve are given so that people have the

A relationship with the Holy Spirit is a golden key in the hand of a Gatekeeper that can open new realms of wealth.

ability needed to excellently fulfill their role in Christ's church.

Gatekeepers play a critical role in the church. The fulfillment of the great commission is the banner the Gatekeeper rallies under. It's the whole meaning behind all of their means and resources. Jesus' last words on earth must be fulfilled (Acts 1:8-9). If God is asking you to dare to be a Gatekeeper—and if your focus is the fulfillment of the great commission—you now know your highest purpose for generating wealth. You will have assets beyond your greatest imagination flow through your hands into the gospel. You will become a portal for the provision of God's work in the earth.

Are you starting to "resonate" yet? Can you "listen to the road?" What's it saying? Is this a challenge you're attracted to? The fact that you are even holding this book in your hands is evidence that God may be asking you to dare to become a Gatekeeper. If He isn't, you probably know someone whom God is daring to rise to the challenge of becoming a Gatekeeper.

Chapter Five

Gatekeepers Turn
Problems Into Promotions

*A*re there specific stories of Gatekeepers in the Bible? Yes there are, and you can learn so much from their successes and failures. Let's look at seven dynamic examples of Gatekeepers.

If you were having coffee with one of them, what would they tell you? If there were one lesson that they learned in life, what would it be? If they could give you one golden secret to their success, what door would it unlock for you? Could their secrets help Gatekeepers today? Let's find out.

Joseph Knew Problems Aren't
Stop Signs—They're Green Lights

If you were the CEO of a Fortune 500 corporation and considering Joseph for a key position in your company, his resumé may read something like this;

Managed family owned business, sold into slavery, retained slave status but promoted to manager of another family owned business, accused of raping wife of employer, incarcerated in prison, retained inmate status but promoted to prison manager, correctly interpreted the dreams of two of Pharaoh's imprisoned staff members, served two more years of prison sentence, exonerated from false rape charge and released from prison early, promoted to interpreter of Pharaoh's dreams, promoted to Agriculture Secretary, promoted to Minister of Finance, promoted to Secretary of the Interior, promoted to Prime Minister of all Egypt, second only to Pharaoh in rank. Wow, what a résumé!

The secret to Joseph's turnaround was solving other people's problems—every problem can create an opportunity for promotion. Many people want their problems to be solved—fewer want to solve the problems of others. "Others" is a key word in the vocabulary of Gatekeepers.

World-class sales expert Zig Ziglar said, "You'll always have everything you want in life if you'll help enough other people get what they want."

Albert Einstein said, "Only a life lived for others is worthwhile."

The most important sign of Joseph's character was that no matter where Joseph was in life—from the pit to the palace—he never stopped being who he was in life. Joseph never stopped solving other people's problems.

Theodore Roosevelt said, "Do what you can, with what you have, where you are."

Joseph never allowed other people's rejections, or his setbacks, to deter him from being faithful with his abilities. Are there rejections and setbacks you've faced that may keep you from being a Gatekeeper? Don't let them keep you from flourishing in the city's gates.

Recently, I read a story about an evangelist I admire a great deal. He visited a large church to minister on a Sunday evening. He said the pastor of the church kept stepping out of the office to check on the size of the gathering crowd. Frustrated with the lack of a good turnout the pastor exclaimed, "I could never preach to a crowd this small!" The evangelist replied, "That's the problem, when you come to

> *A Gatekeeper's circumstances should never deter them from giving their best to others.*

church you expect the people to meet your needs instead of caring about their needs being met. When you care about people's needs being met more than your needs being met, it would matter little whether you preached to two or two thousand." A Gatekeeper's circumstances should never deter them from giving their best to others.

David Yonggi Cho, pastor of the world's largest church, said that during the early days of his ministry, when he used to preach to the few who gathered to hear him in a tattered old army tent, he would close his eyes, imagine a crowd of thousands, and preach his heart out. Cho made a commitment to be who he was in life no matter where he was in life. If you make a commitment to solve other people's problems, no matter what station of life you occupy, you can unlock your promotion to the next level.

> *Treat every person you meet in life as though they're the source for a referral that could take your business to the next level.*

What if Joseph, discouraged that he had been falsely accused and imprisoned, refused to use his ability to manage the prison? It's very likely he never would have met the butler and the baker. He wouldn't have interpreted their dreams, and as a result, he wouldn't have met Pharaoh. Because Joseph was faithful to use his strengths to help others—regardless of his position in life—he met two men that unlocked his next promotion. Treat every person you meet in life as though they're the source for a referral that could take your business to the next level.

Stanley Marcus's father, the founder of Neiman-Marcus, gave Stanley some valuable advice early in his career. A woman with a ruined dress, which she had already worn once, wanted her money back. Stanley argued that they shouldn't do it since the woman had obviously abused the dress. Because of the evidence of wear, it was clear that the manufacturer wouldn't stand behind the piece of clothing. His father reminded him that the woman wasn't doing business with the manufacturer; she was doing business with Neiman-Marcus. His father told him that it didn't matter if it cost them $200 to get a customer and that he refused to lose a customer over a $175 dress. He told Stanley to refund the money with a smile. Over the following years the woman spent over $500,000 at Neiman-Marcus.

I'll never forget a story I heard Pastor Tommy Barnett tell. He was in his study early one Sunday morning preparing for the Sunday service. He heard banging on the door outside and went to find a homeless man wanting food. Tommy could have turned that man down and returned to his study, but above all else Tommy Barnett is a soul winner. Tommy wanted to get this man into church so he could be converted. So, in spite of the interruption, Tommy invited the man to church promising a meal to follow. The man was filthy. Realizing he wouldn't attend church in his present condition, Tommy went home and brought him back a fresh change of clothing. The man attended church and prayed to receive Jesus as his Savior. Eventually this man grew in his Christian faith and went on to live a productive life.

And now, as Paul Harvey says, "Here's the rest of the story . . . ." The man's brother, who was a successful businessman, heard of his formerly homeless brother's conversion and contacted Pastor Tommy Barnett. He was so impressed with his brother's transformation that he gave Tommy Barnett's church their first one million dollar contribution.

Although Pastor Barnett is recognized as a church leader and not a business leader, this story illustrates an important breakthrough principle for Gatekeepers. Treat every person you meet in life as though they will be the source of your next referral. The next person you help in life may not be your big break—but they may know who your big break is. In the same way the homeless man's referral took Pastor Barnett's church to another level, your next referral could break your business into a new level!

Gatekeepers' rewards in this life and the next are determined by their faithfulness in solving the problems they are assigned to solve. Jesus received the biggest reward ever given because He solved the biggest problem mankind has ever had. Paul the apostle said, *"Let this mind be in you, which was also in Christ Jesus: Who… made Himself of no reputation… took upon him the form of a servant… became obedient unto death… Wherefore God also hath highly exalted him, and given him a name which is above every name"* (Phil. 2:5-11).

A Gatekeeper's income is not based on how valuable they think they are—it is actually based on the value of the problems they choose to solve. Money is the result of solving the right problems—if you don't have enough money, you're not solving the right problems for the right people.

Thomas Kinkade, currently the most widely collected living artist, paints pictures of staggering beauty. Every time I look at one his pieces I say to myself, "I want to be in that painting." Somehow, it solves a problem for me—helping me feel a sense of calm in a fast-paced world.

Known as "the painter of light," his paintings have brought this same sense of calm to millions of people. Regardless of your income level, you can enjoy his work and the pleasure of fine art. There are Thomas Kinkade greeting cards, night-lights, blankets, computer screen savers, and books. You can also purchase plain prints of his work, or for much more money, prints that Kinkade has personally "highlighted." For many thousands of dollars, you could even purchase a Thomas Kinkade original. Thomas Kinkade has solved many problems, for many different people, in many different markets. As a result, wealth and influence have been created for him and many generations of his family.

7 Questions To Ask About The Problems You're Solving

1. Do you make more solutions than problems? As best selling author John Mason said, "You will only be remembered for two things in life, the problems you solve and the problems you make."

2. Do you make life more pleasant and meaningful for others, or do you make life more difficult and less meaningful for others? King Solomon said, *"Confidence in an unfaithful man in time of trouble is like a broken tooth, and a foot out of joint"*(Prov. 25:19). Have you ever noticed that when your tooth hurts your whole body hurts? One problem maker can cause pain for a whole organization.

3. What problems are you avoiding that you should be solving? Remember David? He solved a problem everyone else was avoiding and he received a gigantic reward everyone else missed.

4. Are you faithful in solving problems that may seem insignificant? David had to deliver lunch to his brothers before he could meet Goliath. Faithfulness in solving smaller problems precedes larger opportunities.

5. Can you help solve a problem for an influential person? When you do, it will quickly and exponentially increase the number of people you are helping. When Joseph solved Pharaoh's problem he also solved the problem of a whole nation.

6. Is there something you could do right now to increase the number of people you are solving problems for? Jesus said, *"And whosoever of you will be the chiefest, shall be servant of all"* (Mark 10:44). The more people you serve in life, the greater you can become in life.

7. Are there people of resource who could benefit from your solutions? Remember Joseph, a simple man with an administrative gift, who solved

a problem for a man of great resource-the pharaoh of Egypt.

These are questions of self-examination—there are no right and wrong answers. However, they should cause you to think about the quality and quantity of the problems you're solving for others. Remember, your rewards in life are directly proportionate to the problems you solve.

> *Wealth finds its way to people who have solutions.*

The more problems you solve, the more rewards you will receive. The more important the problem you solve, the more important the reward you will receive.

Just like Joseph, your God-given assignment in life is determined to a great extent by the problems you are called, willing, and equipped to solve for others.

As a Gatekeeper, the primary focus of anything you employ yourself with should be solving a problem for another person—you don't need someone to give you a job—you need to solve somebody's problem. Wealth finds its way to people who have solutions. Make a quality decision to have a problem solving mindset.

63

A nobody can become a somebody the minute they solve a problem. David the shepherd boy was a "no-name," then he solved one problem and became a "big-name." After David solved Israel's most gigantic problem, here's what they said about him,

> *Gatekeepers seek problems more than they seek ease.*
> *Ease gives you comfort—solved problems give you rewards.*

"*When David was returned from the slaughter of the Philistine... the women came out of all cities of Israel, singing and dancing... with joy, and with instruments of music... as they played, and said, Saul hath slain his thousands, and David his ten thousands*" (1 Sam. 18:1-8). One day David was singing songs about others. The day after he solved a problem, others were singing songs about David. Solving gigantic problems can give you gigantic rewards.

Gatekeepers seek problems more than they seek ease. Ease gives you comfort—solved problems give you rewards—you need rewards more than you need comfort. As John Maxwell says, "You can pay now and play later, or you can play now and pay later, but all of us will eventually pay."

How does a Gatekeeper know which problems they're supposed to solve? As I listen to many people describe what they believe is their God-given assignment, I am often surprised to find out it has nothing to do with others.

Remember Joseph was committed to helping other people in every circumstance of his life. So are Gatekeepers. Here are seven questions that will help give you clues to finding the problems you're destined to solve.

7 Clues to Help Solve
The Mystery of Your Assignment

1. What problems of others make you the most angry or sad?

2. What solutions do you provide that make you the most joyful?

3. What problems would you solve if money were no object?

4. What would you solve for others if time were not an issue?

5. What problems would you solve for others if you could live for three generations? Many great men and women of the Bible chose to solve problems that would take them more than one lifetime to solve. God is multi-generational. The Bible calls Him, "The God of Abraham, Isaac, and Jacob" (Luke 20:37). King Solomon said, *"A good man leaves an inheritance to his children's children"* (Prov. 13:22). When you can't solve your assigned problem in one life-time, you will leave your children with a greater sense of purpose in their lifetime. What task are you leaving your children to finish?

6. Where would you need to live geographically to complete your assignment? If money really were no object you could live anywhere.

7. If you can't do it yourself—how can you help another do it? Many people are waiting for some magic day to come when they can do

everything they want in life all at once. Is there a reason you can't start helping someone right now?

During his lifetime Walt Disney was famous for his staggering imagination. However, after his death his imaginative ideas live on. The reason is because he made detailed notes and drawings of everything he envisioned. Even if it takes you several sittings, you should sit down and note the answers to the above questions. As a Gatekeeper, it's time to begin to define the problems you are chosen to solve.

Chapter Six

Gatekeepers Know
Mentorship Increases Momentum

During the time in history in which the Queen of Sheba lived, she was the most powerful woman in the world. She controlled a vital trade route near what is now the modern state of Yemen. Spices, precious metals, and other commodities transported throughout the Middle East and beyond, were all conveyed on the trade route within her domain. During her lifetime, the Queen of Sheba was the most successful businesswoman in the world. She also had a great deal of skepticism regarding the success of other business leaders. Her mindset seemed to be, "If you can do it, I can do it too." As a result, she was not immediately impressed when she heard of the greatness of King Solomon and traveled to Jerusalem to scrutinize his ability.

Gatekeepers must realize that no matter what degree of greatness they've achieved, the need for mentorship and coaching is still important to their ongoing success. Gatekeepers need mentors at every level of success they achieve. No matter how great your momentum is right now, keep increasing momentum.

Even the greatest baseball players, home-run hitters like Mark McGuire and Barry Bonds, still have batting coaches. Michael Jordan, the most outstanding basketball player of the twentieth century, still had a shooting coach. Why? Because great achievers still want to keep increasing their performance.

Tiger Woods, one of the best golfers in history, has a coach. Tiger's coach isn't on the PGA tour as a player. Tiger's coach couldn't outplay him. Why does Tiger employ him? Because his coach has an expert grasp on the fundamentals of golf. He can also objectively view Tiger's performance with a view to improving it. He can watch Tiger's game from a perspective that Tiger cannot, both while he is playing and practicing, and then give Tiger feedback critical to his improvement.

When the Queen of Sheba encountered Solomon, she encountered a mentor worth pursuing. Suddenly, she was confronted with someone who had a better grasp on wisdom and success than she did. There should be mentors in your life—people that are qualified to help coach you to greater effectiveness. So many times Gatekeepers have asked me, "How do I know when a mentor is worth pursuing?" The answer to that question lies in the qualities that the Queen of Sheba saw in Solomon. Those qualities made him a mentor worth pursuing.

First of all, the Bible says Solomon answered all of her questions, that *"there was no secret which he did not make clear"* (1 Kings 10:3). Solomon had a grasp of the fundamentals. The Hebrew word translated as "secret" actually means "matter." Solomon was able to tell the Queen what really mattered. A mentor should be able to help clarify the mysteries of your life, by telling you what matters most.

Secondly, it says the Queen saw Solomon's wisdom. Wisdom can be seen. Wisdom is more than just knowing something. Solomon used three important words in his writings to help define wisdom. These words are wisdom, knowledge,

> *A mentor should have tangible proof in their life that they are wise.*

and understanding. Knowledge is the facts.
Understanding is the comprehension of the facts.
Wisdom is applying in a practical way the facts that
you understand. Wisdom is applying the word of God
to your life. When you know something and apply it,
it's wisdom that can be seen. When you start applying
God's word, others will know. The Queen saw
Solomon's wisdom. A mentor should have tangible
proof in their life that they are wise.

What are some of those tangible proofs? The
Bible lists seven tangible proofs of Solomon's wisdom.

1. Solomon built something worthy of respect and
   attention. Likewise, there should be something
   about what your potential mentor is building
   that tells you if he or she is worthy of pursuit.

2. Solomon could provide for many people in his
   household. There was always meat on Solomon's
   table. There should be something about the provision that a mentor enjoys, and provides for
   others, that gives you insight about his ability.

3. Solomon's servants were organized. Is there a sense of rank and order in the workforce of your potential mentor? Do the employees of your potential mentor benefit from their association in that workforce?

4. Solomon recognized people's talents and empowered them to serve others. Are the employees of your potential mentor being properly utilized for their ultimate effectiveness?

5. Solomon's employees were well dressed. How do the employees of your potential mentor present themselves in professional encounters?

6. Solomon employed wine bearers who brought celebration into the day. I've been told there is an old Jewish saying used at weddings and celebrations, "Where there is no wine, there is no joy." Solomon wanted a joyful environment to surround him. Are there people in your potential mentor's organization that dispense joy and a sense of humor?

7. Solomon sacrificed many burnt offerings. Are your potential mentors givers? Is there an aroma of generosity about their life? Do they give in a way that inspires others to action?

The Bible says after the Queen witnessed these things there was *"no more spirit in her"* (1 Kings 10:5). When you observe these qualities in a person whose mentorship you are pursuing, are they evidenced in a sufficient degree that it takes your breath away? Are you left speechless? If so, then that person qualifies as a mentor worthy of pursuit.

These aren't easy qualifications to live up to. Not everyone is going to have it all together in all seven areas. However, one thing is fixed. You can be certain about the safety and worth of a mentor by observing the people under their direct influence and in the organization that they lead. The Queen observed that Solomon's wives and servants "were happy." As a

> *The people in your potential mentor's family and organization are a mirror of your mentor's true wisdom and ability.*

result, she noted that they were blessed. The people in your potential mentor's family and organization are a mirror of your mentor's true wisdom and ability.

The Bible also says that at the end of the Queen's encounter with Solomon, Solomon gave the Queen more than she had given him. A mentor that increases your momentum always causes you to depart with more than when you came.

Although a mentor must be pursued, and the responsibility for pursuit is always upon the protégé, you will always leave the presence of a mentor more enriched than whatever it cost you to receive their mentorship.

Chapter Seven

Gatekeepers Know
Patience Doubles Outcome

*T*elephone books are filled with business names that use the words "quick," "speedy," and "minute." Domino's delivers fresh, hot pizza in under an hour. Jiffy Lube offers ten-minute oil changes. The U.S. Postal service is now known as "snail mail." In today's marketplace, patience may be a virtue but it's certainly not a commodity.

Does patience really have a place in the life of a Gatekeeper? I'll have to admit, one of my favorite words is "now," one my least favorite things is being stuck in the iron claw of gridlock, and even the name of my church is Today's Church.™ However, the story of Job has great insight for us in this fast paced world of instant gratification.

Job was a man who took his whole life to build an impressive family owned and operated business.

Then in two days it was all gone—his business, his wealth, his family, everything. The book of Job is the story of how Job regained his lost wealth and went on to enjoy it with his great grandchildren.

The life of Job contains some of the Bible's most important lessons on wealth. Yet Job's life is, without a doubt, one of the most misunderstood and controversial lives in the Bible. Many feel the book of Job is a story of judgment—portraying God as an oppressor. Nothing could be further from the truth. The book of Job is a story of God's love, and one man's determination to serve God, regardless of satanic opposition or the difficulty of his circumstances.

The real story of the book of Job is a message resulting in a victorious final outcome—how one man lost everything and then regained double what was lost. One real key to success is quickly rebounding from loss. Some Bible scholars have said that Job doubled his outcome in only two years. The real story of Job is summed up in it's final passage, *"And the LORD turned the captivity of Job, when he prayed for his friends: also the LORD gave Job twice as much as he had before"* (Job 42:10-17).What was Job's secret of success? Let's find out. Thirty-five chapters of the book of Job record detailed conversations between Job and his "friends." These conversations describe Job's journey of patience through pain.

Think about it—thirty-five chapters. It's amazing how much time is given describing Job's conversation with his "friends." I believe the Bible is trying to tell Gatekeepers that when you face difficulty and pain, one of the most time consuming elements will be dealing correctly with those closest to you. One of the most important things you can do when under attack is guard your conversations.

> *Experiencing pain doesn't make you a great leader, but all great leaders have experienced and overcome pain in their life.*

Another important lesson from Job is that you will have to endure difficulty without giving up in order to fulfill your calling and be successful. Experiencing pain doesn't make you a great leader, but all great leaders have experienced and overcome pain in their life.

Winston Churchill's father struggled with ill health due to venereal disease. His mother was exceedingly immoral and had adulterous relationships with many of the business and political leaders of Europe. When he was a young man his grandmother told him to "give up this foolishness of writing." Yet, Winston Churchill was one of the greatest political leaders of the twentieth century and a prolific writer who wrote many volumes of books and articles. One of Churchill's shortest and greatest speeches was, "Never, never, never, give up." All great leaders have overcome pain in their life.

> *To break into unimaginable realms of wealth, Gatekeepers will have to overcome pain.*

When you think of overcoming pain you should think of the story of this man's timeline:

- Age 22, failed in business
- Age 23, ran for legislature, but was defeated
- Age 24, failed again in business

- Age 25, elected to legislature
- Age 26, sweetheart died
- Age 27, had a nervous breakdown
- Age 29, defeated for speaker
- Age 31, defeated for elector
- Age 34, defeated for congress
- Age 37, elected for congress
- Age 39, defeated for congress
- Age 46, defeated for senate
- Age 47, defeated for vice president
- Age 49, defeated for senate
- Age 51, elected president of the United States

This is the story of Abraham Lincoln. Because he never quit, he won the highest office in America.

Henry Ford failed in every other business effort aside from the automobile industry.

> *If your enemy believed that wealth would destroy you, he would have given it to you long ago.*

He went broke in the automobile industry five times before he succeeded.

To break into unimaginable realms of wealth, Gatekeepers will have to overcome pain. If your enemy believed that wealth would destroy you, he would have given it to you long ago.

Job's patience was the golden secret that helped him overcome the pain he faced. Patience is more than just having the ability to not become angry in a difficult situation. Patience is the power that will carry you through the painful moments of life into the pleasurable moments of life.

The writer of the book of Hebrews says of patience, *"That ye be not slothful, but followers of them who through faith and patience inherit the promises"* (Heb. 6:12). The day your patience runs out is also the day your faith will run out. A Gatekeeper's faith level will never exceed his patience level.

At times Job was pressured by his pain to run away from God. Patience was what kept Job in the proper place until he could experience all that God had promised. Patience helped Job stay put until he doubled his outcome. Patience will help you stay invested when you feel like cashing out.

Patience is what keeps the seed of your faith planted until you have an appointment with your harvest. Faith plus patience equals an inheritance—faith minus patience equals nothing. When you lose your patience you will never find your promise.

The Greek word translated as patience means, "to be long in spirit or to be long in passion." Patience is doing what God's word says is right longer than your problems can stand it. Sufficient exposure to the word

The patience of God within you will always outlast the pain that's trying to come upon you.

of God and the Holy Spirit before, during, and after crises will increase your patience (Gal. 5:22). The patience of God within you will always outlast the pain that's trying to come upon you.

Patience is the power that will keep you in the proper place and mindset, during discomfort or pain, until you possess your final promise and reach your ultimate purpose.

Pain may not always be an indication that something is wrong. Pain can be evidence of a properly implemented strategy that is now being opposed. When pain tries to serve you with an eviction notice mark it, "RETURN TO SENDER." History is filled with people who triumphed over pain.

Bury him in the snows of Valley Forge with no warm clothing, and you have George Washington.

Raise him in complete poverty with no formal education, and you have Abraham Lincoln.

Deafen a maestro composer with his prime years before him, and you have Ludwig van Beethoven.

Have him born of victims of a Nazi Death Camp, his body paralyzed with a crippling condition from the waist down at age four, and you have concert violinist Itzhak Perlman.

Call him slow, retarded, unable to concentrate, with no hope of being properly educated, and you have Albert Einstein.

Four Things Gatekeepers Should Know About Pain

When you encounter painful times in life there are four things you can learn from Job.

1. You can't always prevent pain from happening, unless it is self-inflicted, but you can always prevent it from stopping you.

2. Your final outcome is much too wonderful to never enjoy because of pain.

3. Pain, properly endured and overcome, prepares you to mend another's wounds. Compassion for others, resulting from overcoming pain, can take you to new realms of influence and help further identify God's usefulness for your life.

4. When in pain ask "what questions" not "why questions." Ask questions like, "*What* is the next step to fulfill my dreams"?

Many people begin to ask, "Why me?" when they should be asking "What now?" The question, "God, *why* did this happen?" only breeds uncertainty in the midst of pain. Uncertainty breeds doubt. Doubt is a barren wasteland without an oasis.

Instead pray, "God, if there is something I could have done to prevent this show me when I'm ready to know the answer." Then, aggressively move ahead to fulfill your dreams unencumbered with self-doubt.

Chapter Eight

Gatekeepers Turn Adversities Into Profits

*J*acob worked for an unjust employer. His employer, Laban, defrauded Jacob of promised wages—not once or twice, but on ten different occasions. Laban built his wealth on the back of Jacob's efforts and then refused to reward Jacob appropriately. Have you ever faced an adversity like that? Are you making your company a great deal of money, but experience little or no reward? You may own your business, have a client whom you've helped a great deal, and they've not compensated you appropriately. Your enemy doesn't really have any new tricks. He still uses the same tactics to try and undermine the business ventures of Gatekeepers.

Jacob exercised extraordinary creativity during his adversity. As a result, he dramatically increased his profits. Jacob went from working the farm to owning

87

the farm. Laban's efforts to limit Jacob were ineffective, and like a boomerang, they actually ended up turning back to harm him.

God gave Jacob a creative idea that revolutionized his industry. Jacob's ingenious idea created a new system of animal husbandry. Jacob was even capable of engaging his new profit-making system while he slept.

> *Creativity is taking what you uniquely possess and doing something unanticipated, unexpected, and extraordinary with it.*

Do you have a system of wealth creation that will work when you don't and cause checks to keep coming in the mail even when you're sleeping? Jacob did—and God helped him to develop it.

Even if you're in the midst of adversity, such as Jacob experienced, you can still increase your profits. Creativity is the key. Creativity is taking what you uniquely possess and doing something unanticipated, unexpected, and extraordinary with it. Creativity can start with a little and end with a lot.

Gatekeepers in adversity, who need to increase their wealth quickly, must unlock the power of creativity. Let me share a creativity-boosting Bible verse with you.

> *But thou shalt remember the LORD thy God: for it is he that giveth thee power to get wealth, that he may establish his covenant which he sware unto thy fathers, as it is this day* (Deut. 8:18).

How does God create wealth for Gatekeepers? He doesn't. It's the Gatekeepers responsibility to create wealth. In Deuteronomy, the Hebrew word translated as *get* means, *"to create."* What did God give you? God gave you power to create wealth—He doesn't create it, you do.

How? Gatekeepers are seers. They see things differently. They're always looking for potential opportunities where others see problems. Jacob saw herds of spotted livestock when everyone else saw Jacob as an hourly wage earner. God helped Jacob see the potential in his situation, even when it seemed like a dead-end street.

Ivar Haglund, founder of the famous "Ivar's Fish & Chips" restaurant chain in the Pacific Northwest, had a problem when he opened his first store in downtown Seattle. One day, on the railroad track in front of his little fish and chips stand, a train derailed and spilled a tanker of maple syrup all over the roadway. No one could access his store. It would take days to clean up. Ivar knew he was in trouble. Then an idea struck. Ivar ordered all of his employees to go out and buy all of the pancake mix they could find. Ivar's Restaurant began to serve free pancakes, along with the maple syrup from the spilled tanker, to anyone who would come to his restaurant. The media heavily covered his pancake feed and Ivar received thousands of dollars of free advertising. From that day forward Ivar conducted numerous publicity stunts that went on to make "Ivar's" one of the most famous restaurants Seattle. Ivar saw potential where everyone else saw a problem—he took his unique situation and did something unanticipated, unexpected, and extraordinary.

Be a prophet of potential. See possibilities in your circumstances. When you look for potential, creativity can take something that is worth nothing and make it worth something.

Isaiah the prophet said, *"God will give you the hidden riches of secret places"* (Isa. 45:3). Are hidden riches waiting to be discovered right under your nose?

Charles Goodyear purchased an India rubber life preserver as a curiosity. He had a feeling that something very useful could be made of rubber. Once, when someone inquired where they could find Goodyear, they were told, "Look for a man with a rubber hat, a rubber coat, rubber shoes, and a rubber purse in his pocket with not a cent in it—that is Charles Goodyear." As you know, Goodyear's belief that rubber had potential eventually paid off in a very big way.

Creativity is also released when we ask the right questions. It is appropriate to question everything when you ask questions with the right attitude. Have you ever noticed there were two different sets of questions posed to the angel who foretold the supernat-

> *Creativity is also released when we ask the right questions.*

ural births of Jesus and John the Baptist? Mary posed one of them. She asked, "How can this be, Lord?" The angel answered her question without incident. The father of John the Baptist posed the other. He also asked, "How can this be, Lord?" He experienced a completely different outcome and was struck mute. The questions seem identical, but the difference was their attitudes. Even though the questions had the same words, they had a different intent. One of them was a question of exploration. The other was a question of doubt. Questions of discovery and exploration open us up to God's assistance. Questions of doubt close us to God's assistance.

Some of the world's most successful people have asked questions of exploration.

Albert Einstein asked, "What would a light wave look like to someone keeping pace with it?"

Bill Bowerman, the creator of Nike shoes, asked, "What would happen if I pour rubber into my waffle iron?"

Fred Smith, the founder of Federal Express, asked, "Why can't there be a reliable, overnight mail service?"

Godfrey Huntsville, the inventor of the CAT scan, asked, "Why can't we see in three dimensions what is inside of a human body without cutting it open?"

Mashura Abuca, the chairman of Sony, asked, "Why don't we remove the recording function and speaker from a tape recorder, make it small and put headphones on it?"

History records some of the responses to these questions. Most of the other shoe companies thought Bowerman's waffle iron idea was "really stupid." So, when he was trying to sell his waffle-iron-bottom shoes to other companies, no one wanted it. He had to start his own company, which he called Nike. It is now obviously one of the most successful athletic shoe companies in the world.

Godfrey Huntsville was told that the CAT scan was impractical and unnecessary. Mashura Abuca received comments like, "A recorder with no speaker... and no recorder. Are you crazy?" Yet, it turned into a device called the Walkman, and as you know, the Walkman has changed the way we listen to music. Fred Smith, who proposed the idea of Federal Express in his business class at Yale, received a "C" on the paper he wrote about it.

During periods of great change, answers usually don't last, but questions do. It is going to take tremendous creativity from Gatekeepers to create wealth in these times of constant change. God wants to give you that creative power.

Questions that release creativity are open-ended. Begin to ask questions like, "What would it be like if I poured rubber into my waffle iron?" Or like Jacob, "I wonder what would happen if I put a spotted stick in front of a pregnant cow?"

Chapter Nine

Gatekeepers Have a
Multiplication Mindset

Abraham is the only Bible character described as "very rich." That is quite staggering when you consider the almost incomprehensible wealth of some of the other figures in scripture. Abraham was the only individual in the Bible known to have his own personal army. Abraham had three hundred and eighteen employees that were cross-trained as soldiers. Genesis says they were born from the other servants in his organization, so Abraham obviously had many more employees than just his soldiers. He literally had to support a whole caravan of people who complimented and sustained his small army. I wonder how much food three hundred soldiers eat every day? My two sons alone drink almost a gallon of milk daily. With his army, Abraham actually defeated the combined armies of four different regions. They must have been a highly trained and equipped group of soldiers.

Abraham was also diversified. The book of Genesis says he was very rich in three different commodities. Evidently Abraham didn't believe in putting all of his eggs in one basket, although all of his baskets were heavily guarded. What would Abraham tell a Gatekeeper today? What could you learn from his success?

Abraham was a big thinker. God had trained Abraham to think in terms of multiplication. God told Abraham when he was without an heir, *"I want to multiply you"* (Gen. 22:17).Then God did something awesome. He gave Abraham three object lessons to train him to have a multiplication mindset.

First, God changed his name to "father of nations." Not nation. Nations. Abraham didn't have even one son, and now he was supposed to go around and ask all those employees to begin to address him as "father of nations."

Next, God told him every time he looked at the sand it would represent how many offspring he was going to have. Then, God told him every time he looked at the stars they would represent how many offspring he was going to have. That's a lot of kids and grandkids.

Abraham didn't have one child—not one. Yet that was when God wanted him to think in terms of multitudes of children. Everywhere he looked, day and night, he saw multiplication. Every time he heard his name he heard multiplication. Every time he said his name he talked multiplication.

If you want multiplication in your business, you must first put multiplication in your eyes, ears, and mouth.

When you need addition God will train you to think in terms of multiplication. To train you to think in terms of multiplication, God will ask you to change what you're seeing, hearing, and saying. Gatekeepers see things, hear things, and say things everyday that encourages their dream to multiply.

A lead story in a Seattle newspaper once read, "MEN BECOME ILL WHILE SIPHONING GAS." The article went on to tell the story of two men trying to illegally siphon fuel from a large RV. Instead of the fuel tank, the men mistakenly inserted a hose in the RV's septic tank and accidentally ingested it's contents.

The wrong input will produce the wrong results. In a similar manner, the same input produces the same results, and new input produces new results. Do you want new and better results in life? Begin to change what you see, hear, and say.

Walt Disney was fired from several jobs as a young man. Many of his former employers said young Walt was a dreamer who wouldn't amount to anything. Walt constantly created images, drawings, and models of his fantasies. He also seemed to talk endlessly about his ideas. He continually saw, heard, and said his dreams. Today, long after his death, "imagineers" at Walt Disney World are still using his dreams to make new additions to the mammoth entertainment company.

> *God multiplies any equation he becomes a part of.*

If you want multiplication in your business, you must first put multiplication in your eyes, ears, and mouth.

As a Gatekeeper you must learn God's math system. You plus you equals zero. You plus God equals mega multitudes. God multiplies any equation he becomes a part of. Seeing what God wants you to see, hearing what God wants you to hear, and saying what God wants you to say, puts him in the equations of your life.

One businessman, who had recently accepted Jesus as his Lord, wanted God to be a part of his business equation so badly that he actually had his lawyer draw up papers showing God as his senior partner. The written agreement entitled God to a majority of the profits. The following year his business multiplied.

Rolls and Royce became partners. So did Procter and Gamble. There is also Hewlett and Packard, just to name a few. How about you and God? There are two gauges of God's partnership in your business. Firstly, are you constantly thinking bigger? Secondly, is God blessing you with multiplication? If he's involved, you'll eventually do both and it all starts in your eyes, ears, and mouth.

How else can a Gatekeeper involve God in their business activities? Abraham brought ten percent of the spoils of the battle he'd won to God. The Bible calls the practice of giving ten percent of your increase "tithing." It also clearly states that your entire tithe is to be brought as a gift to your house of worship (Mal. 3:10).

The act of providing first for what spiritually sustains you, shows that you realize there is a Source beyond your human ability to create increase in your business. Tithing demonstrates that you believe your financial well-being is tied to your spiritual well-being.

There is another benefit of tithing. When give the first ten percent of your money away, you are training your sub-conscious that you already have more than enough money for everything else. You've now added tithing as another weapon in the arsenal of expanding your mindset.

God's kingdom needs Gatekeepers that are big thinkers. Paul Harvey said, "I've never seen any monuments erected for pessimists." But there are monuments the all over world honoring big thinkers. Henry Ford said, "A man can always do more than he thinks he can." So think big. Paul the apostle said, *"God will do superabundantly more than you dare think"* (Eph. 3:20, Amplified). The bigger you think the more God will exceed your thinking.

Chapter Ten

Gatekeepers Value People More Than Money

*T*o this point, King Solomon still holds the record for being the richest man who ever lived. Solomon wasn't a billionaire, he was a trillionaire. His riches exceeded the combined riches of all the kings who were his contemporaries. Solomon's house alone, which took thirteen years to build, could be valued in modern currency at more than $500 billion dollars. Now that's a house! As for Solomon's pastimes, his stables housed forty thousand of the finest Arabian horses—they could easily be valued today at more than $400 million dollars. Basketball superstar Michael Jordan would have to work ten years, at his highest salary, to afford the horses in Solomon's stables. The stables Solomon built for his horses were so magnificent that their ruins can still be visited almost 4,000 years later. Even Solomon's name means "peace." The Hebrew concept of peace isn't the absence of antagonism. It's the ability to build, sustain, and enjoy wealth and health in spite of antagonism.

In the light of such mind boggling wealth, is there a message in the life of Solomon for Gatekeepers? How did he tap such magnificent resources? What were his secrets?

Most importantly, Solomon valued people more than he valued money, recognition, or honor. Because Solomon cherished the people under his influence, it unlocked wisdom from God so he could properly fulfill his role as their leader.

God came to Solomon in a dream one night. He told Solomon he could ask for anything he wanted. Solomon could have written his own ticket with God. What would you have asked for?

Unlike what many of us have been told, Solomon did not just ask for wisdom in general. He asked, "Lord give me a heart that will understand the principles I need to correctly value and lead your people." Solomon realized that his assignment, the people of Israel, were a sacred trust and he asked God for wisdom to treat the people correctly.

Solomon longed to fulfill his assignment in a manner that benefited God's people. Solomon cared about God's people more than anything else. He could have asked God for anything, but he valued people most.

I remember having my mother read me the story of King Solomon many times when I was a little child. As I lay in bed at night, she would tell me the stories of Solomon's childhood, his wealth, and influence. Then she would ask, "Nate, what do you want to ask God to give you tonight before you go to sleep?" Now after having heard the story of Solomon so many times I knew the "right answer" was wisdom. But I really didn't want wisdom—I wanted a dog and a new bicycle. Nevertheless, I'd answer "wisdom" and mom and I would pray for it before I went to sleep. I asked for it because I thought I should.

Solomon asked for wisdom because it was what he really wanted—not just wisdom in general—he longed for the ability to correctly handle God's most precious possession, His people.

God's response was staggering. First of all, God responded to Solomon's words. Sometimes I wonder if the many things we often ask for merit a response from

God. The book of James says, *"You have not because you ask not and when you ask you do so with the wrong motivations"* (James 4:2-3).

Solomon's motives were in line with God's heart and God responded to his prayer.

Secondly, God liberally gave Solomon the wisdom he needed. The book of First Kings goes on to tell us Solomon had more insight than the sand on the seashore and more wisdom than all of the scholars in Egypt. Think about the engineering marvels of ancient Egypt, and yet Solomon's wisdom exceeded it all. Solomon spoke three thousand proverbs and wrote over one thousand songs. He understood science, biology, agriculture, and botany. All the kings of the earth came to hear his wisdom.

Thirdly, God made him completely unique among his contemporaries. There was not one other king like him. With wisdom God could make your business completely unique—there could be no one else like you.

Fourthly, God gave Solomon great stature among those with a similar assignment. He was a leader in his field. Others sought him as a mentor.

Finally, God gave Solomon riches and length of days. Solomon not only enjoyed wealth, but he also enjoyed good health. All of this came because he valued people more than money.

Immediately prior to Solomon's dream he gave God an offering that would be worth well over two hundred thousand dollars today. You might think, "Well, he was the richest man in the world; he could afford it." But Solomon gave that gift before he was the world's richest man. Solomon valued people and he valued pleasing God. He valued it more than money even before he was the world's richest man. It was a golden key that unlocked greater wealth for him.

> *When you value people and pleasing God more than money, it changes how you look at money.*

When you value people and pleasing God more than money, it changes how you look at money. Money becomes a means to an end instead of an end in itself. When gathering money isn't your future, you're free to use your money to release your future. Your money needs a greater assignment than just accumulation. Solomon invested money in his dreams. He knew money alone wasn't his assignment—it was just a tool to help him fulfill it.

Whenever Solomon gave to God, no matter how wealthy he became, his gifts were always large enough to move his heart. That kind of giving kept Solomon in a place of humble receptivity to God's voice. In Solomon's case, money was truly his servant and not a master.

In the early days of Solomon's reign he didn't value the opinions of men as much as the opinion of God. He wanted to be honored by God more than he wanted to be honored by men. Solomon didn't let the praises of people go to his head any more than he let their criticisms touch his heart.

It can be difficult to know how you'll respond to people's praise until you actually receive their accolades. One way to understand how you may respond to praise is to consider how you currently respond to criticism. I remember being very discouraged after hearing some harsh criticisms of myself. A friend of mine made a very insightful comment. He said, "Nate if you take people's criticism personally, it's an indication that you'll also receive their praise personally." Your critics aren't taking you too seriously—are you taking your critics too seriously?

An old Chinese proverb says, "Man who says it can not be done, should not interrupt man doing it."

A wise person knows that the people who can't dance always say the band can't play. It's thousands of times easier to criticize something than to create something. Critics never contribute. Critics aren't interested in helping people solve problems, they're only interested in pointing people's problems out. You owe critics nothing, so never pay them by responding.

Another old proverb says, "Critics are like men with no legs trying to teach other men how to run." Don't let legless critics run your life.

The foundations of Solomon's peaceful reign were his desires to help people and receive honor from God. Gatekeepers must possess the same guiding values if they want to tap the unimaginable wealth of Solomon.

Chapter Eleven

Gatekeepers Know Money Can't Be Trusted

$\mathcal{M}$ost people see wealth as an opportunity for greater freedom. But in the gospel's story of the rich young ruler, wealth proved to be a limitation. I have always been amazed by the story of this successful young businessman's encounter with Jesus. Jesus asked thirteen men to follow him. Twelve of them answered, "yes." One of them answered, "no." Peter, James, and John all said "yes" but the rich young ruler said "no." Why? Is there something about money that could cause someone to say no to Jesus? Is there something deceitful about wealth that could trick you into living a limited life?

In the gospel of Mark, Jesus coined a very powerful phrase—the phrase is, "the deceitfulness of riches" (Mark 4:19). The most deceitful thing about money is that it appears to be trustworthy. The deceit lurks in the feelings of security that money can provide.

Paul told his young protégé, Timothy,

> *"Challenge those that are rich in this world, that they be not high-minded, nor trust in uncertain riches, but in the living God, who gives us richly all things to enjoy."*

1 Timothy. 6:17

Why did Paul say riches were uncertain? To be uncertain means to lack full assurance. Money can't provide people with complete assurance. Money doesn't give total certainty, safety, or stability.

Rush Limbaugh, a politically conservative radio personality, is one the most successful people in the media industry. Although sometimes controversial, his success in radio broadcasting is unprecedented. By Rush's own admission, he's achieved enough success in his field that he'll never have to think about money again. Sadly, Rush experienced a terrible crisis in his health. He became almost totally deaf in a matter of just a few weeks. Rush is now fighting a battle to try and recover from his seemingly incurable hearing loss.

Christopher Reeves, the famous actor who portrayed the comic book hero Superman, was paralyzed after being thrown from a horse. He now battles to regain his mobility and lobbies for greater research to be done for those with spinal injuries.

Ralph Waldo Emerson said, "The first wealth is health."

Trust in God is like a shield against the devastating impact of life's tragedies (Eph. 6:16). However, wealth cannot insulate a person from unforeseen calamity. Even wealthy people can face devastating crises. In many cases, their money can do little or nothing to actually solve their problems. Sadly, money may only provide things that ease their pain. As one wealthy person once put it, "Money hasn't made me any happier, it's just made me less miserable."

The famous boxer Joe Louis once said, "I don't like money actually, but it quiets my nerves."

The rich young businessman wasn't a bad person. In fact, he was spiritually hungry. The scriptures say he came to Jesus wanting to know how to have eternal life. The gospels record that the young businessman had obeyed the scriptures from his childhood.

However, in spite of all those pluses the rich young ruler had one big minus. His sense of reliance was in his money more than God. The rich young ruler needed to transfer his trust to God.

Wealth is always a test of trust. The more wealth you have, the more you will have to put your trust in God. To the person who has difficulty relying on God, wealth seems to make God unnecessary. Gatekeepers know money is a poor substitute for God.

Paul told young Timothy that the rich should not be "high-minded." To be high-minded means to be of a high opinion of yourself, to be self-elevated, and self exalted. When people put their reliance in money, they elevate themselves inappropriately in their own minds. They elevate themselves to place of seeming safety.

When people put their trust in money, instead of God, it warps their character. World famous author F. Scott Fitzgerald said,

Let me tell you about the very rich. They are different from you and me. They possess and enjoy early, and it does something to them, makes them soft where we are hard, and cynical where we are trustful, in a way, that unless you were born rich, is difficult to understand. They think, deep in their hearts, that they are better than we are because we had to discover the compensations and refuges of life for ourselves. Even when they enter deep into or world, or sink below us, they still think that they are better than we are.

The cure for people in this condition is to realize that it is God who gives us richly all things to enjoy. When you know God is your Source, you also know that money isn't your source.

Giving is always a way of transferring trust back to God. To solve the rich young businessman's trust problem, Jesus asked him to sow a seed that was beyond his imagination. Jesus said, *"sell all you have and give it to the poor"* (Luke 18:22). Later, Peter's reaction was, "Lord we've left all to follow you." Jesus replied that whomever left anything for the gospel would receive a one hundred fold return of whatever they left, both in this life and the one to come, accompanied by persecutions.

Jesus wanted the young businessman to trust God as his Source of supply. Jesus gave this young businessman an invitation to live a life where the pressures of finance and business have less impact—a life where his trust had been transferred to God.

Unfortunately, the rich young businessman missed out on his opportunity to be a Gatekeeper. Astonishingly, he said no to the greatest opportunity of his life. He decided he'd rather keep what he had, than receive more than he'd ever known.

That's why Gatekeepers should always be striving to give more than ever before. It will launch you from one level of trust to another. Giving keeps you from hitting a trust plateau.

Gatekeepers keep the resources flowing. As more wealth comes to you, keep it flowing through you. It must become your lifestyle. Gatekeepers live to give, and give to live.

Chapter Twelve

A Gatekeeper's Call To Action

*I*f God is asking you to dare to be a Gatekeeper, you must decide that you want it more deeply than any alternative.

Richard Petty has made more money than any other stock car driver in history. However, listen to the story of when he reported the results of his first race to his mother.

Young Richard Petty rushed into the house shouting, "Mama, there were thirty five cars that started, and I came in second place in the race."

His mother replied, "You lost."

"But mama, don't you think it's pretty good to come in second place in my first race—especially with so many starters?"

She said, "Richard, you don't have to run second place to anybody!"

For the next twenty years Richard Petty dominated the world of stock car racing.

The words, "Richard, you don't have to run second place to anybody!" rang in his mind all those years.

You must make a decision that being a Gatekeeper isn't going to come second place to other business goals. Being a Gatekeeper is your greatest business success. You don't have to run second place to anybody.

It's never too late to start. Bill Walsh, former head of the San Francisco 49ers, is considered to be an offensive master. So why did Bill Walsh have to have gray hair before the NFL recognized his ability? Walsh said, "I was forty-five years old before I even had an interview for a head coaching job in the NFL." And then he didn't get it. He was turned down.

> *You must have the will to win at being a Gatekeeper.*

He was interviewed by the Bengals. Rejected.

He was interviewed by the Jets. Rejected.

He was interviewed by the Rams. Rejected.

The pros labeled Bill Walsh, "Not a head coach."

But after he was accepted in his first NFL head coaching position and three Super Bowl victories later, Bill Walsh proved that it's never too late to start.

You must have the will to win at being a Gatekeeper. Knute Rockne said, "Some say the will to win is a bad thing. In what way? Success in life goes to the person who competes and wins. A successful lawyer is the one who goes and wins. A successful physician is the one who goes and wins by saving lives. A successful sales manager is someone who goes and wins by making sales. There are no rewards for losing. So that leaves living life only one way—with the will to win!"

Gatekeepers must go out and win. Your enemy is not going to hand you wealth on a silver platter with an apple in its mouth, although he may try to roast you and serve dinner.

As George Ade said, "Anyone can win—unless there happens to be a second entry."

God needs you to go into the city gates and contend for resources to flow into the Kingdom of God.

Theodore Roosevelt said,

The credit belongs to the man who is actually in the arena; whose face is marred by dust and sweat and blood; who strives valiantly; who errs and comes short again and again; who knows the great enthusiasms, the great devotions, and spends himself in a worthy cause; who, at best, knows in the end the triumph of achievement; who, at worst, if he fails, at least fails while daring greatly, so that his place shall never be with those cold and timid souls who know neither victory our defeat.

It's time for Gatekeepers to recognize their abilities and do something.

It's time for Gatekeepers to think big, as Abraham did.

To serve others nobly, as Joseph did.

To value people deeply, as Solomon did.

To sit at the feet of a mentor, as the Queen of Sheba did.

To be cunning and creative, as Jacob was.

To endure pain and overcome, as Job did.

To not miss the opportunity to be a Gatekeeper, as the rich young ruler did.

It's time to act.

A Prayer For Gatekeepers

Dear God, thank You for Your marvelous grace. Thank You that the body of Christ is so diverse and each member functions differently. Thank You that You give each member the ability to function correctly.

I ask You to help me function in my ability as a Gatekeeper. I'm going to the marketplace today and I need to find Your wisdom there. I'll be searching for resources that will help Your work in the earth be accomplished. Please lead me to them today.

Help me to think big and solve other's problems. Help me to value people and be creative. Help me to endure suffering and be patient. Lord, show me the right mentors to listen to.

Lord most of all, help me not to miss any opportunity to be a Gatekeeper. I want to give something to Your work today. I trust You to be the Source for my life. In Jesus Name, Amen.

A Prayer to Receive Jesus As Lord

If you're unsure if your sins have been forgiven, or if you lack certainty that you will go to heaven, please pray this prayer:

Dear God, I know that I have sinned and I need Your help. I now turn from my sin and invite You into my heart and life. I believe in my heart that Jesus Christ died for my sins and that You raised Him from the dead. With my mouth I confess that Jesus Christ is Lord. He is Lord of my life. He is Lord of all. From now on, if I make any mistakes in following Jesus, I won't become discouraged and quit. I will simply ask forgiveness and keep believing in Christ. Please help me to find a good church and strong Christian friends. Thank You for answering my prayer and saving me. In Jesus Name, Amen.

Author Contact Information

To contact the author, receive additional copies of *The Gatekeepers,* or to learn more about The Gatekeepers Network please write, call, or visit on-line at:

Pastor Nate Wolf
10121 Evergreen Way
PMB 632
Everett, WA 98204

1 (888) anointing

www.Gatekeepersnetwork.com